Davies of the Clwyd Valley

A Family History

by

John Barford Lindop

and

Dorothy Lindop née Davies

MERCIANOTES

First published privately by the authors 2000
First published by the Mercianotes 2015

All rights reserved. No part of this publication may be reproduced, stored in a retrieval system, or transmitted, in any form or by any means, electronic, mechanical, photocopying, recording or otherwise, without the prior permission of the publisher in writing. This book is sold subject to the condition that it shall not, by way of trade or otherwise, be lent, resold, hired out, or otherwise circulated without the publisher's consent in any form of binding or cover other than that in which it is published and without a similar condition being imposed on the subsequent purchaser.

John and Dorothy Lindop asserts their moral right to be identified as the compiler of this work in accordance with the Copyright, Designs and Patents Act, 1988.

© *2015 John and Dorothy Lindop*

Mercianotes
Brackenrigg
Wigton
CA7 5AQ
United Kingdom

ISBN: 978-1-905999-23-1

Davies of the Clwyd Valley

A Family History

by
John Barford Lindop
and
Dorothy Lindop née Davies

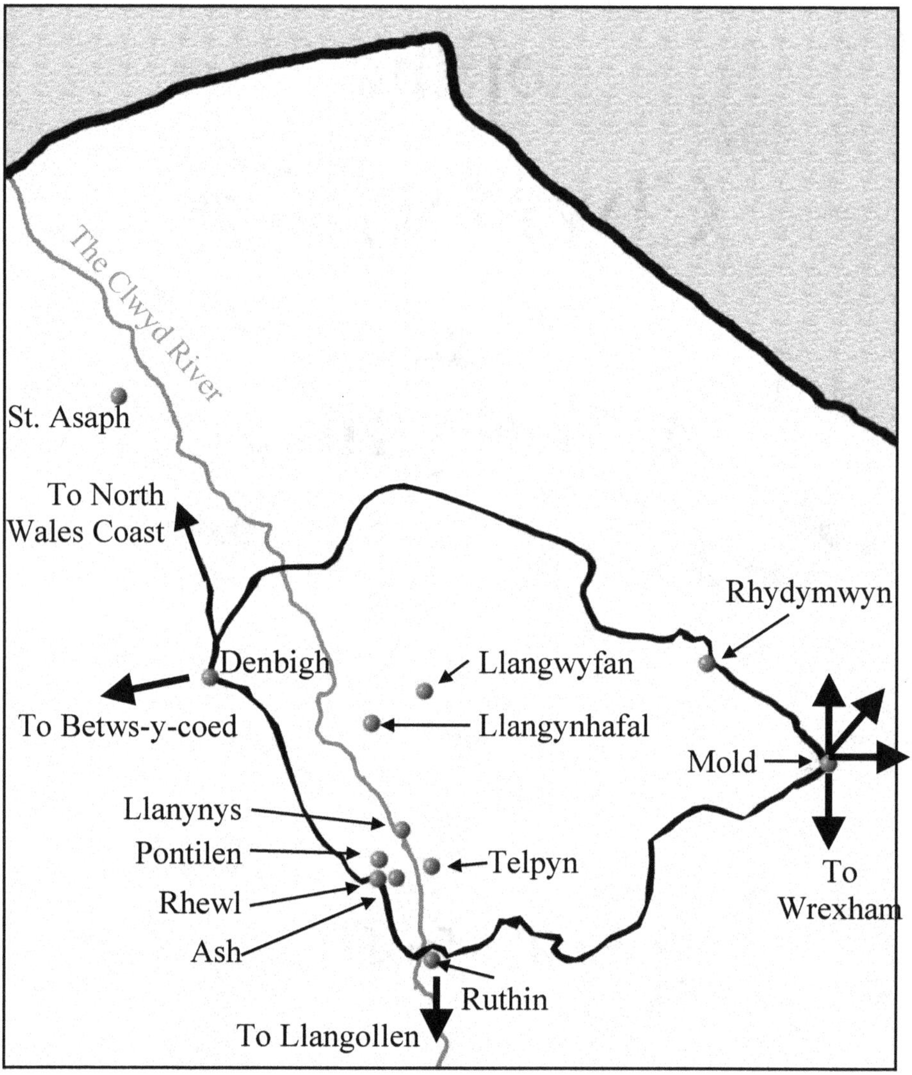

Sketch map of the towns and hamlets discussed showing some of the main roads in the area.

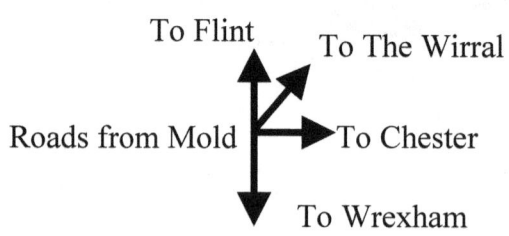
Roads from Mold

Contents

Preface	3
Introduction	5
The Davies Family	7
Aunt Em and Jake	47
Wedding Guests and other relatives	50
Welsh Placenames	54

The guests on this photograph are identified on Page 53

Preface

It was anticipated that tracing the genealogy of the Davies family would be a straight forward exercise in the usual way, however this proved not to be the case as the history of the family, especially in Chester, was inextricably tangled up with the history of the family firm of confectioners, so the research was extended to cover that as well.

This produced a surprise in the form of Robert Jones Davies, of whom none of the present generation had any knowledge at all and, although there was a vague family memory of the Roodee Works and some confectionery activity there, nobody seemed to know who operated it, exactly where it was sited nor where it fitted into the family history.

Robert Jones Davies was crucial, not only to the foundation of the confectionery business but to the actual presence of the Davies family in Chester, all established solely due to his enterprise. It is therefore surprising that a personality of such fundamental importance to the Davies story was apparently quite unknown in recent times and it has taken such an effort to uncover the tale. Hopefully this history will now remedy the omission.

Another point of interest that has emerged from the shades is the highly fortuitous marriage of Amos Jones Davies to Mary Elizabeth ('Polly') Brown. Following the breakup of R. Davies & Co., with Amos Jones and brother Richard going their separate ways, it was evident that the driving force, (i.e. Richard), had been removed. Amos Jones comes down to us as a bit of a romantic with more interest in his books than the family business but, luckily for him and all who followed, it turned out that Polly was a person of great business ability and energy and it seems that it was she who largely built up A. J. Davies & Co. into the successful firm it eventually became.

It is worth mentioning at this point that two rather remarkable pieces of good fortune attended the search, the first was finding a photograph of Robert Jones Davies, and his brother Isaac, improbably found, after all else had failed, hanging on the wall of the Welsh Church in St. John St. Chester. The second was discovering the property where the wedding photograph of Richard Davies and Elizabeth Clegg was taken, being the home of her Uncle, a senior Waterworks Company employee, where she lived. It had eluded being located for some time until chance led to the discovery that it was hidden away from public view in the grounds of the Chester Waterworks Company in Boughton.

It has taken some fourteen years research to get to this point, where the bulk of the history has been discovered, however John, Elizabeth and Mary, children of Isaac and Margaret have not been traced nor William Isaac, John and Ernest, sons of Robert Jones, all of whom may have descendants with vital information, additionally there is the enigma of Polly and Mrs. Brown, so there is still some work to do and hopefully someone in the future can fill in the gaps.

Isaac Davies, posing for his new fangled photograph to be taken for posterity at Connah's Quay sometime about 1880

Introduction

IT IS A strange, if slightly eerie feeling, to stand on the doorstep of a property and know your ancestors stood on this very same spot at Hwlyfa and Pontilen Bach some two hundred and forty years before. One is tempted to wonder about their lives and from their Wills and Inventories we have a good idea how their houses were furnished, what their meagre possessions were, the equipment they had for working the land, the crops they grew and stored in the barn and the clothes they wore, giving us some idea of their appearance. Also, luckily, many of their houses remain so there is little problem from that aspect.

Lives were hard, frugal and sometimes brutal by modern standards, with backbreaking labour from dawn to dusk and a terrifying death rate, especially among the young.

Exactly what those far off Davies ancestors looked like we will never know though a clue does survive in the photo, believed to be Isaac Davies, posing for his new fangled photograph to be taken for posterity at Connah's Quay sometime about 1880. He wears the clothes of a working man, probably an agricultural labourer like his ancestors and he doesn't look too happy at the experience. If he was Isaac Davies, although we cannot be sure, he was born at Telpyn in 1851, youngest child of Isaac and Margaret Davies. We do not know why he thought his photograph should be taken but it was included in the family treasures so there must have been some cogent reason, now lost alas.

With his characteristic Welsh features he strongly resembles Lizzie and Maggie and others of the Davies family, so clearly a very close relation.

The area of research where all these remote ancestors were born, worked and lived out their lives is close to Rhewl, near Ruthin, North Wales, an area with a population density and distribution little changed from that of two or three hundred years ago.

It is a part of the countryside that has hardly altered at all in hundreds of years and, in that respect, we are fortunate indeed that it has not disappeared under a supermarket carpark or housing estate.

Even Isaac's great-great-great-great-great-grandparents, Richard and Catherine, who lived somewhere in Rhos, Llanhychan Parish *circa* 1695 would, if they somehow came back today, have little trouble in recognising the rural environment, the roads, lanes, villages, mills, houses, farms and churches they once knew so well.

From a genealogical standpoint we are also lucky in that, by rule of thumb, if one manages to struggle back to 1750 in Wales, an area notorious for the very restricted number of surnames, one is considered very lucky indeed.

Research in the Rhewl area revealed that, so far as could be determined, those Davies found were all members of our family group, even if some of them were very distant indeed, so the job was a bit easier than it might have been, although there were problems enough.

Today the family has not moved all that far from the origins in the Vale of Clwyd, with the striking and dominating view of Moel Fammau, for that Bald Mother Mountain is still clearly visible, if from the English side of the border.

In all this research one thing is very evident in that of all the properties once occupied by various elements of the Davies family in Chester, nearly all of them have been demolished, mostly in the great slum clearances and road building programmes of the immediate post World War II period, and today the merest handful remain.

Nobody can say what Robert Jones, Amos and Ellen and all the others of the Davies family would have thought of the changes we have wrought, but there is little doubt that few of them would have approved of what we have managed to do to our once fair City, much of it wanton and needless destruction of swathes of our once rich historical heritage in the name of progress and the ubiquitous motor vehicle.

Of those who have assisted in the research for this history special thanks are due to The Chester Record Office, the Chester Register Office, The Cheshire County Record Office, L-P Archaeology, Denbigh Record Office, Denbigh Register Office, Blacks Research Service, Mrs. G.D. Thompson of Liverpool, Lynne Gardiner of *Lost and Found*, that expert on Welsh genealogy Daffyd Hayes of Gwernymynydd, Martin Wheeler for help with the McLellans and, of course, all those members of the family, and others, who have been thoughtful enough to keep material of an historic nature and who have passed on family tales for the benefit of posterity.

Without all their help this work would not have been possible.

John & Dorothy Lindop,
Duddon Common, Tarporley.
March 2010.

The Davies Family

IT IS more than probable that the Davies ancestors had lived in the general area around Rhewl (2.5 kms. to the NNW of Ruthin, North Wales) for generations, possibly for hundreds of years before first appearing in the records although their racial origins were probably the Celts from Europe.

The earliest known record of a Davies ancestor appears in the Church Register for Llanhychan Parish and is a Richard Davies who married Catherine sometime around 1698.

Unfortunately the wedding cannot be traced, it may have taken place in Llanhychan Parish Church but the first surviving complete Register dates from 1700 and, though Bishop's Transcripts exist from 1676, many are missing and the marriage may well have occurred in one of the missing dates.

Maybe Catherine came from another Parish and the wedding took place in the traditional way. There are several Richard and Catherine weddings in the area but it is not certain which, if any, is ours :

Richard Davies = Katherine Woodnett,	Bangor is y Coed	1694
Richard Davies = Katherine Jones,	Llanelwy, St. Asaph	1693
Richard Davies = Caterine Williams,	Abergle	1695
Richard Davies = Katherine Thomas,	Llandygai	1693
Richard Davies = Katherine Pierce,	Llandygai	1696

Perhaps they were Non Conformists or whatever, of which there is some later evidence, or decided to marry at home after assembling the required number of witnesses, this being before the days of the Marriage Act: perhaps they didn't marry at all.

Llanhychan surely must be the smallest Parish in Wales, being a mere 567 acres and a population in 1885 of 85 persons grouped round Rhos, so probably fewer in 1698.

It seems likely that Richard would have been an agricultural labourer, (*i.e.* farm worker), like most of the community in those times, he probably lived in Rhos or nearby, working on one of the local farms or estates and more than likely living in a tied cottage with a few acres for his own use; there is a strong chance the property is still there.

He probably attended Llanhychan Parish Church, still operating and in excellent condition as is the National School next door, where many of the Davies family must have been educated. Richard and Catherine had eight children, only three of whom survived childhood, one only just, as the Llanhychan Parish Register records :

Maria	born 22 March 1699	
Elizabeth	born 3 March 1702	died 20 April 1722
Robert	born 19 May 1706	died 1 May 1709.
Catherine	born 17 April 1709	died 24 May 1709
Catherine	born 17 September 1710	died 4 February 1711
David	born 26 January 1711	died 29 March 1712
Richard	born 14 July 1713	died 29 October 1785
Robert	born 4 January 1717	died 12 April 1718

A harrowing mortality rate, not untypical of the times with minimal medical and surgical care to deal with diphtheria, smallpox, typhus, cholera, asthma, measles, scarlet fever and malnutrition being the worst childhood killers.

Richard seems to have died late in the year of 1728 without leaving a Will, by no means unusual as tradition determined that the Estate usually went to the wife or eldest son. However he did leave an Inventory so we have some idea of the lifestyle on his smallholding of two or three acres which amounted to In all £25.0.0.

item	£	s	d
Sheep	2	0	0
2 Cows	3	0	0
2 Mares	3	0	0
2 Pigges		10	0
Hay	1	0	0
Oates & Barley	1	10	0
Peace		5	0
Carl		10	0
Harrow		5	0
Boards	1	0	0
Brass, Pewter & all household goods	12	0	0
TOTAL	25	0	0

Peace was an alternative spelling for peas, an important source of winter feed and grown in conjunction with Oates; Carl (an English dialect word) was Hemp and grown as a cash crop for sale to ropemakers, an important product in the days of sailing ships.

The Inventory was taken in November so the crops must have been in store in the barn. There is a Letter of Administration signed by Catherine Ellis and Griffiths Jones, the latter named on the Inventory, so they were probably neighbours and suggesting that Catherine had died before Richard and there was some problem in settling the Estate.

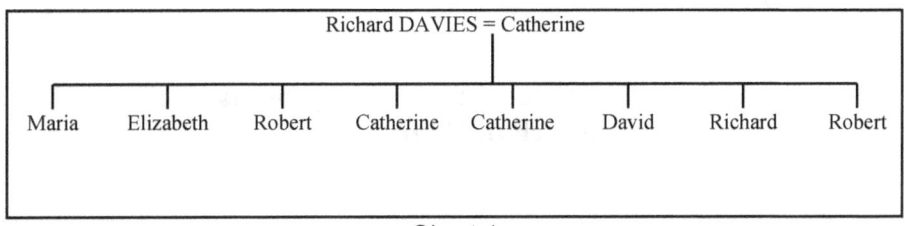

Chart 1

It must be noted that a query arises at this point in that there appears to have been more than one Davies family in Llanhychan Parish, possibly even in Rhos, no doubt all closely related:

23 November 1728, Richard Davies, buried.
6 December 1747, Richard, son to Rich'd Davies was buried.
16 September 1762, Richard Davies was buried.
9 August 1772, Sarah Davies, widow of Rich'd Davies was buried.

Llanhychan Parish Church

The Churchwardens Accounts for Llanhychan have many Richard Davies entries, some of them probably ours, though it is not possible to tell which is which from available evidence. However, the information is an interesting insight into life in the parish at that time:

Extracts from The Churchwardens Accounts for Llanhychan Church

1744 paid Rich'd Davies for Shooting 2 woodpeckers & to jo Edw'ds for a pole Catt £0: 1: 8d.

paid Rich'd Davies for ye Highway warr't. £0: 1: 0d.

1746 paid Rich'd Davies for a Highway war't at Trevechan £0: 2: 0d

1749 Richard Davies & John Jones Churchwardens.

1750 Richard Davies for a load of stones, £0: 0: 4d

1756 The mark of Rich'd Davies RD (signed as churchwarden)

1757 Ditto.

David Griffiths paid to Richard Davies his success what by ye warr't appeared to be ye Ballance of his acco't ye sum £51: 15:11d.

1756 paid for 3 High Way warr'ts to witt to Da Pierce, Wm Parry and Rich'd Davies 2p each 0: 6 : 0

1757 The acco't of Richard Davies late Ch; Warden of Llanynis

1758 1762, 1763 (RD signs as churchwarden)

1763 December 19th and ordered the Richard Davies late of pen y craig shall Have one shilling a week until further ord'r....

1754 June 18 a Day attending Mr. Yale on Rich'd Davies acc't £0: 1 : 0

1771 Arrill [April] 28th A list of ye poor that receive weekly Allowances on the upper Townships (Bryncaredig)

Richard Davies £0: 1 : 0

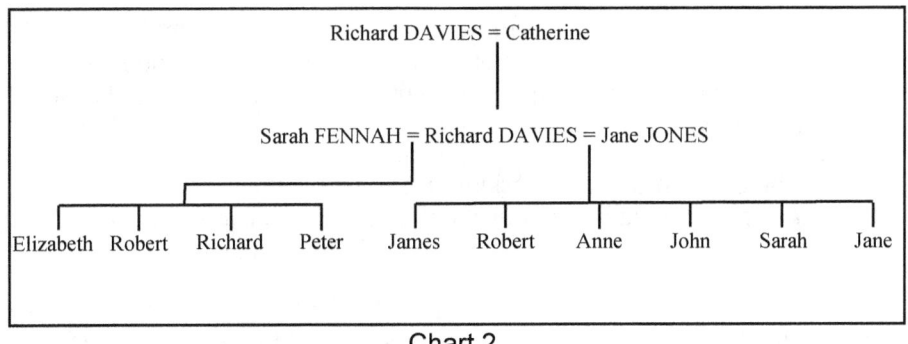

Chart 2

It should be noted that the law required all legal documents, Church records and so on, to be in English, something that must have presented formidable problems to a completely Welsh speaking society as few, other than perhaps the local Doctor and Clergy, could speak English.

The direct ancestor was Richard, (born 14 July 1713), and he married, by licence, Sarah Fennah at Hope Parish Church on 14 January 1743 and more than likely lived at Rhos as had his parents, maybe taking over their employment and smallholding in the traditional manner.

There were four children of the marriage, all born and baptised at Llanhychan:

Elizabeth	24 Nov 1744.
Robert	27 March 1746 to 6 December 1747
Richard	4 October 1750 to 29 October 1785
Peter	20 October 1753

It appears that Sarah died sometime following the birth of Peter, maybe as a consequence of the birth, always risky in those far off times, but no burial can be found for her, if indeed it was recorded.

Richard remarried at his Parish Church of Llanynys. The record describes him as a widower of Maesmaencymro township, who married by Licence, Jane Jones of Llanfurog on 20th. June 1760.

Llanynys Parish Register records the following Baptisms to Richard Davies, labourer, of Maesmaencynro township and Jane his wife:

James	20 July 1760.
Robert	13 September 1761.
Anne	16 September 1764.
John	2 April 1768.
Sarah	1 February 1772.
Jane	29 May 1774, buried the same day.

To cloud the picture a bit there were two Richard Davies and Jane marriages in Llanynys in 1760, the other being Richard Davies and Jane Roberts, married by Banns 17 May 1760, but if they remained in the Parish there is no evidence they had any children.

If all the children of Richard, widower, and Jane formed a family group there must have been rather a houseful though by no means unusual to have ten or more children to compensate for the terrible child mortality rate.

According to the Register the family lived at Pontilen where there are two smallholdings, Hwylfa and Pontilen Bach, both probably tied to the large Estate at Pontilen where Richard most probably worked.

Hwylfa

There is some indication that the family lived at both addresses as the Register records births at both properties.

These cottages, tied to the employment, were usually set in two or three acres with a barn and outbuildings for the use of the occupant and produced a useful return for maintaining the family in the form of winter fodder for the animals, (cows, sheep, pigs, poultry and so forth), also grain for baking and brewing, milk for butter and cheese and Hemp as a cash crop for raising some money, so the unit was largely self supporting in most consumer items.

Both the properties have survived, Hwylfa much modernised but Pontilen Bach retaining much more of the original structures.

Of the various children of Richard and Jane the direct ancestor was John, recorded as being Baptised 2 April 1768.

As an Agricultural Labourer and living in Llanynys Parish, most probably still at Hwylfa, he married Elizabeth Roberts, by Banns, at her Parish Church of Llandyrnog on 28 April 1793 and they had five children, all apparently born at Hwylfa:

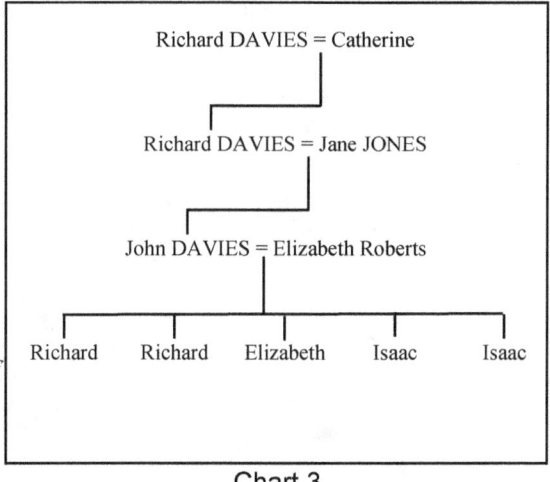

Chart 3

Richard	13 April 1794.	Isaac	21 June 1802.
Richard	3 July 1796.	Isaac	24 February 1805.
Elizabeth	25 December 1798.		

Pontilen Bach

Rhewl Church

Llanynys Church

Llyndyrnog Church

Elizabeth died 14 January 1841 aged 78 and John 18 May 1847 aged 80, both are almost certainly buried at Llanynys but the graves cannot now be traced.

Of Isaac, (born 24 February 1805), who is the

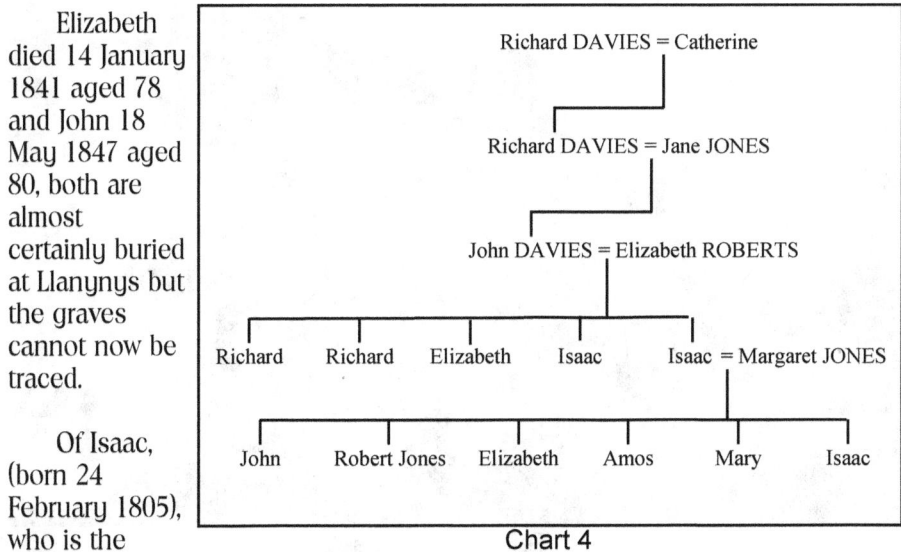

Chart 4

direct ancestor, a good deal more is known and he sounds an enterprising sort of chap who had much improved his position from earlier times as an agricultural labourer. He is variously described as a labourer in 1832 and a farmer of five acres on the 1861 and 1871 census returns. On the census of 1881 he is additionally described as a coal Merchant.

Isaac married a five months pregnant Margaret Jones of Llanfair Duffryn at her Parish Church on 30 May 1832 and they clearly continued the Davies occupancy at Hwylfa as their first four children were born there and Baptised at Llanynys Parish Church:

	baptised	buried
John	28 October 1832.	
Robert Jones	25 December 1835	3 August 1910.
Elizabeth	19 August 1838.	
Amos	2 February 1841	8 November 1907.
Mary	1846.	
Isaac	1851.	

Following the birth of Amos the family must have changed employment as the next child, Mary, was born at Llyngynhafal and the last child, Isaac, was born at Telpyn.

Their address was 1, Telpyn Cottages, which have changed hardly at all since built, possibly in the 17th century, maybe even earlier, being a terrace of small stone cottages probably built for Agricultural Labourers on some local Estate.

Around the 1851 period there were, confusingly, three Davies families living there, most likely all closely related, Isaac as above plus Richard Davies a Tailor and his wife Elizabeth and children Elizar, John and Naomi.

Telpyn Cottages

Additionally there was Elinor Davies, a pauper widow and probably a Davies-in-law with children Margaret, Jane and Edward and most likely living on Parish Relief and the charity of relations. By the census of 1871 Isaac and Margaret and family had moved to Telpyn Farm, a small two story Victorian farm built onto the end of the terrace of Telpyn Cottages and with direct access to the fields beyond which formed the five acre farm and still clearly identifiable as such. From that property the coal merchant business was also conducted.

Isaac died Feb. 12th 1892 aged 87 without leaving a will and Margaret died in 1894, also aged 87, both are buried in Rhewl churchyard a short distance from their home at Telpyn. Interestingly a Davies was still living in Telpyn Cottages until recent times and certainly a member of our Davies group and, if not a near relation, there are close connections. His great great grandfather was John Davies born in Cyfflliog and living at Llanfwrog, and was the manager of a mineral water factory, probably in Ruthin, and there may be a link here with D.C. Davies who operated a mineral water factory in Chester called Dee Cestrian & Laycock; he had two daughters living in Chester with whom Aunt Emily was very friendly. John Davies' father was Evan Thomas Davies, (born 2nd March 1878), and his father James Davies, both of whom worked for Uncle Isaac at Melin y Wern at Ash, just down the road from Telpyn. Isaac and Margaret's son Robert Jones was obviously a chap of considerable business ability and on the 1861 Census he was recorded as a traveller in confectionery, presumably for a firm in Ruthin, where there were several such, and his occupation eventually led to the founding of the various Davies confectionery businesses in Chester; R. J. Davies & Co., The Chester Preserving Company, A. Davies & Co., R. Davies & Co., A. J. Davies & Co. Ltd and The Deva Confectionery Co. Ltd.

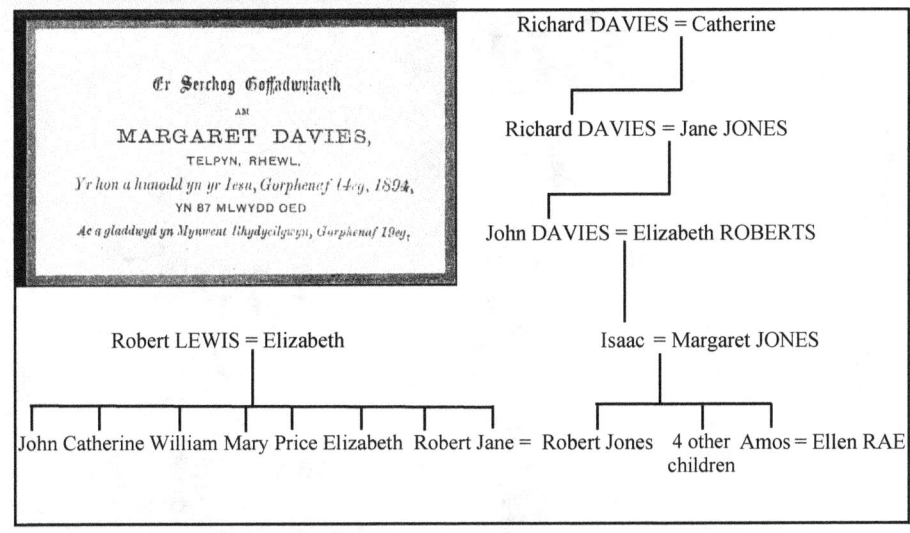

Chart 5

On 3rd May 1865 Robert Jones Davies, officially resident at Telpyn, (despite the press report noting he came from Liverpool, married Jane Lewis of The Cross Keys, Llanycil near Bala, she was born 2nd December 1844.

At the time of the wedding she was living at 3, The Groves, Chester (now Number 12) and the ceremony took place at the parish church of St. John's, Chester. Jane's parents were Robert Lewis, an innkeeper of The Cross Keys, Llanycil, (born Llanycil in 1806), and his wife Elizabeth, (born Llanfor in 1806), there was the usual large family:

John, born 1829,
Catherine, born 1831,
William, born 1833,
Mary, born 1835,
Price, born 1837,
Elizabeth, born 1840,
Jane, born 1844,
and Robert born 1854 (out of sequence on the chart).

Telpyn Farm

Amos & Ellen Family Grave   Isaac & Margaret Family Grave

In addition to being an innkeeper Robert was also recorded on the 1851 Census as being a farmer of five acres, presumably attached to the Inn and maybe this is where he grew crops for the production of beer etc., a common practice at the time.

Also on the 1851 Census were :
Elizabeth, wife, aged 48,
William, son, aged 17,
Price, son, aged 13,
Elizabeth, daughter, aged 10,
Jane, daughter, aged 7
and Catherine Jones, a lodger, char woman, aged 50.

Robert Jones Davies gave his age as 29 on the marriage certificate whereas he was 33, a popular dodge to reduce the age gap between husband and wife.

By the time of the wedding Jane's father had died, sometime between 1853 and the 1861 census, so her mother signs as witness, also so did Morris Jones, a name we will meet again.

Following their wedding Robert Jones and Jane made their home at 3, The Groves, a very large double fronted Georgian styled property, a far cry from the small stone cottage where he was born.

The property has had many functions over the years; Deva Cottage, when a private house, later Deva Hotel, Deva Cafe until recently, and presently, Deva House, a private domicile again though renumbered to Number Twelve when many new houses were built in The Groves in the mid 1870s. The first three children were born at 3, The Groves, the family being listed there in the 1871 Chester Trade Directory, however, they evidently moved that year to 3, Hoole Park, a large Georgian house similar in size and status to 3, The Groves.

At around the time of the wedding Robert Jones Davies evidently founded the confectionery business of R. J. Davies & Co., listed in various Chester trade directories as manufacturing confectioners, with premises at Star Court, 32, Cuppin Street, Chester, property to the rear of and rented from The Star Inn.

Why he selected that site is not known, it may have been a random choice with good access, acceptable rent, available space and so on but perhaps a clue exists in that opposite The Star Inn was once one of Chester's three sugar houses and boiling sugar was much the same as producing boiled sweets and though closed when Robert Jones Davies arrived, maybe the equipment was still there, for things changed slowly in those days.

Whether Robert Jones Davies had partners in the enterprise from the foundation of the Company is not known, but there were certainly two such who tendered their resignation in 1883, John Rowlands Edwards and Elizabeth Edwards.

3, The Groves, Chester

3, Hoole Park

Also completed in 1866 was the Welsh Calvanistic Methodist Church in St. John St, Chester where Robert Jones Davies was to play such an important part as a Deacon and where all his children were baptised. His funeral service was also held there.

1871 was seemingly a busy year for Robert Jones Davies and the census return for 3, Hoole Park lists :

Robert Jones, head, aged 35, manufacturing confectioner.
Jane, wife, aged 27.
Margaret Elizabeth, daur, aged, 4
William Isaac,   son, aged 3,
Mary Catherine, daur, aged 11 months.
Isaac, brother, aged 20.
Marie Edmonds, servant aged 26 from Bangor.

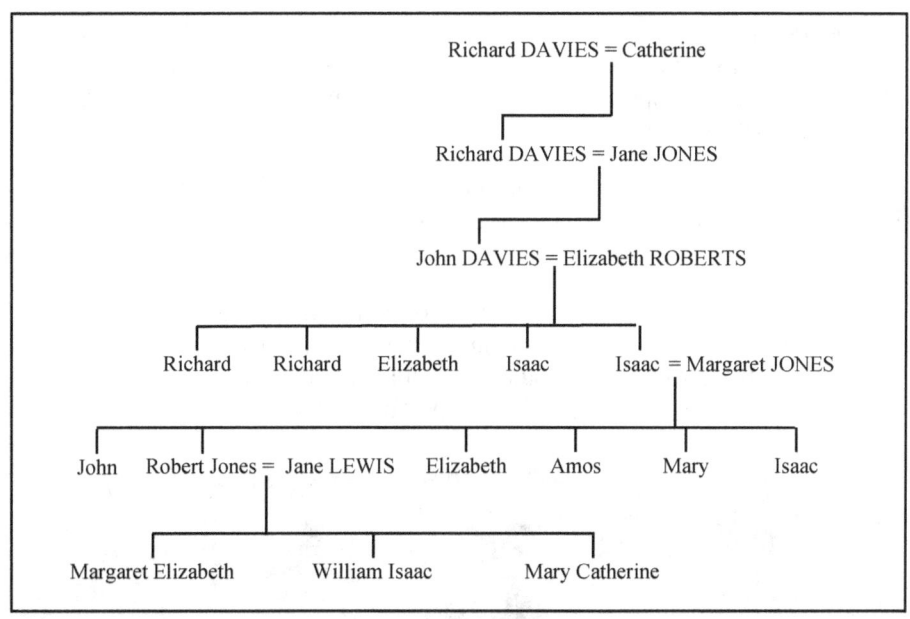

Chart 6

Clergy and Elders, Welsh Church, St. John Street, Chester circa 1900

Robert Jones Davies back row second from right.and his brother Isaac is next to him at the end of the row.

On 1st March 1873 Robert Jones Davies, in partnership with Richard Hitchen, farmer of Hurleston, signed a lease for a shop in Cynwyn, which had apparently been a drapers, but why they took it over is not recorded, perhaps for another sweet shop.

1877 saw a major expansion in the fortunes of the Company when Robert Jones Davies moved from Cuppin Street to take over the Roodee Steam Works, a now defunct title for a steam cleaning process for heavy fabrics.

The 1878 Chester Trade Directory records that R. J. Davies & Co., Wholesale & Export Confectioners, had moved into the Roodee Steam Works, which was rented from the Chester City Council, and commenced manufacturing confectionery, with the operation titled the Chester Preserving Company (Roodee Works).

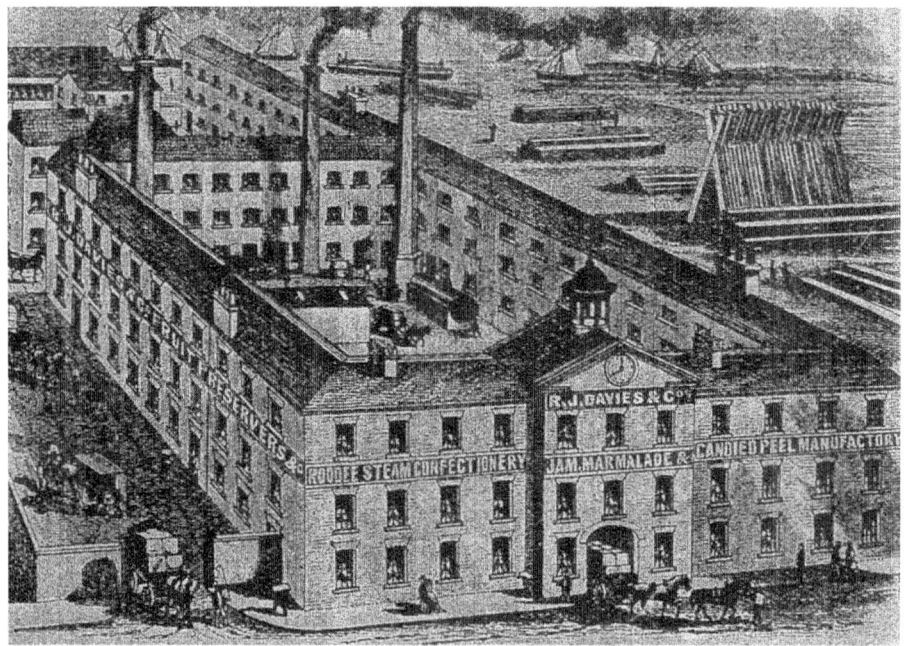

Roodee Works

So Robert Jones Davies was also making preserves, as jam was then known, the only way then for preserving soft fruit, blackcurrants, strawberries, plumbs etc., in addition they also made Candied Peel and sugar confections for table decorations, popular in that period.

The property the Company had moved into in the newly named Kitchen Street was one of the largest buildings in Chester, previously the Chester Union Workhouse. The House of Industry, (as the Workhouse was also known), was a building constructed in 1759 at a cost of £1,500, replacing the many small workhouses previously operated by the nine individual Parishes in Chester, with great multiplicity of effort, so an obvious administrative and

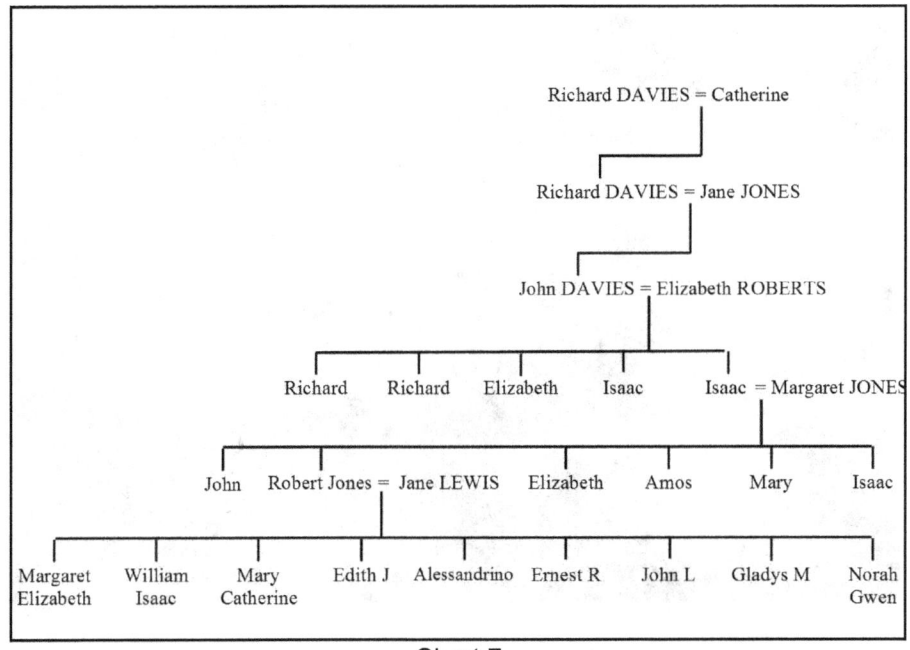

Chart 7

financial improvement. On 24th February 1767 the building was completely destroyed by a fire which started in the cotton processing section, burning to death fifty persons, including thirty children; the property was eventually rebuilt.

The fire of 1767 seems to have started a rumour that the same thing happened again circa 1905, but the building was demolished in the normal manner. The Workhouse in Kitchen Street was left vacant when the new Workhouse was constructed in Hoole, later the City Hospital, now demolished.

On 20th September 1900 the Liverpool Mercury reported that the Chester City Council had agreed to sell the old Workhouse building and adjacent land, which they called the Roodee Jam Factory, in Kitchen Street, to the Chester Gas Company for the sum of £5,000.

The property last appears in Kelly's Directory for 1902 and is no longer listed in 1906, having been demolished during the previous years; a new gasholder was built on a part of the site in 1909. In 2005 L-P Archaeology carried out an extensive excavation and published a comprehensive report on the site of the old Workhouse and Chester Preserving Company and found much evidence of sweet-making in the form of glass jar lids etc.

The jam and confectionery business must have been brisk although, unfortunately, we do not know how profitable all this effort was as no such records have survived. However the 1881 Census Return for 3, Hoole Park

14, Eaton Rd.

records Robert Jones Davies, aged 45, Manufacturing Confectioner & Fruit Preserver employing 21 men and 22 women and boys, so an operation of some substance. Also in the household (see chart 7) :

    Jane, aged 37,   Mary, 10; daughter
    William Isaac son, aged 13,   Edith, 9; daughter
    Isaac, brother. Commercial Clerk (Confectionery), suggesting he looked after the administrative affairs of the Company
    plus a General Servant, Elizabeth Gagen,
    and a Monthly Nurse, Hannah Sproston from Chester, aged 55,
    plus a Nurse / Servant, Sarah Jones, aged 15 from Llanfairfechan.

The Monthly Nurse was a Maternity Nurse, known as the Monthly, who lived in the household for that period, part prior to, and part following, the delivery. The Chester Directory for 1886 records the family still at 3, Hoole Park but the 1891 Census Return shows they had moved house to 14, Eaton Road, Handbridge.

However, between moving from 3, Hoole Park to 14, Eaton Road, in 1890 the family was living at 32, Duke Street for an unknown period; the property was demolished in recent times and replaced by a new building.

    The 1891 Census Return for 14, Eaton Road, Handbridge :
    Robert Jones aged 55, Manager, Confectionery & Jam Works
    Jane M. aged 47, wife   Ernest R. aged 14, son
    Margaret E. aged 24, daughter   John L. aged 12, son
    William I. aged 23, son   Gladys M. aged 8, daughter
    Edith J. aged 19, daughter   Margaret Jones aged 19, Servant.
    Alesandrina aged 16, daughter

This does not record Norah Gwendoline who died aged 11 months on 31st January 1887 and the matter of the Monthly on the 1881 Census is not resolved as no child of an appropriate age appears on the 1891 Census, nor in the family grave, so perhaps it was premature or stillborn.

Brother Isaac Jones is no longer with the family and had moved on to marry Emily Ginever from Hagley on 1st November 1881 and received a present of a marble clock, which is still in the family, suitably engraved

> "Presented to Isaac J. Davies on his marriage
> from his fellow employees, Roodee Works,
> November 1st. 1881".

He set up home at 28, Cambrian Crescent, (renamed Gladstone Road), Chester and on the 1891 Census he is noted as a Commercial Traveller, presumably for the Roodee Works and they had children : Herbert, Muriel, Margaret, Harry and Phyllis.

Following the 1891 Census the family moved to Croydon and the 1901 Census notes three further three children were born there: Arthur, Bernard and Frederic.

Left to Right: Gladys, Margaret, Jane, Alessandrina, Mary, Edith

Isaac, assisted by his wife Emily and daughter Muriel, set up and ran a laundry at his home at 21, Decimus Burton Road, Thornton Heath, Croydon. Isaac died in December 1928 and is buried at Mitcham Road Cemetary, Croydon.

The 1891 Census for the Roodee Works, Kitchen Street shows confectionery was still being made there with a Williams family in residence as caretakers: Edward Richard Williams, aged 26, Warehouseman, Jam & Confectionery Works plus his wife Mary aged 33 with three step-children and one son, aged 6 months. Also resident was John Morris Jones, aged 23 from Wales, Manager, Confectionery & Jam Works. Additionally, there were several lodgers, all from Wales.

Kellys Directory of Chester for 1892 records the Chester Preserving Company at Paradise Row Roodee and operated by David Jones & Co. now Robert Jones Davies's employers and where he evidently remained as Manager to pass on the appropriate skills prior to moving on.

16 Eaton Road

Throughout the history of the various Davies enterprises nearly all involved were Welsh. Sometime later in the year of 1891 the family seems to have moved from 14, Eaton Road to next door at 16, Eaton Road, Handbridge, where Robert Jones Davies is noted on the 1901 Census as a Commercial Traveller.

Robert Jones Davies, having retired from his final position as Manager of the Roodee Works and now employed as a Commercial Traveller by David Jones & Co. of Liverpool, wholesale fruit merchants and possibly the suppliers of some of the fruit for the Roodee Works. As a Rep. for David Jones & Co. now the owners of the Roodee Works, it is likely that Robert Jones Davies was again Travelling for what had been his own business.

The 1901 Census lists three children (see Chart 7) still at home:
Margaret aged 34, School Governess;
Edith, aged 26, also School Governess
and John, aged 22, Assistant Manager, Jam & Sweet Works, (so there was still some family influence at the Roodee Works),
plus two servants, Margaret Jones, aged 21
and Susanah Manuel, aged 18, both from Wales,

and two lodgers : Henry M. Mather, aged 49, a Bank Cashier and A. Hamilton Price, an Inspector of the Board of Agriculture, so respectable middle class professional people.

It is clear that substantial social and employment changes had occurred in the Robert Jones Davies lifestyle, his reduction to Manger, then back to his old job as a Commercial Traveller, taking in lodgers then compounded by the fact that his wife, Jane, was going out to work and is recorded in the 1892 Chester Trade Directory as having a Ladies Outfitters at 5, Northgate Row, utilising in part the sweet-shop latterly owned by the Company and now operated by her Brother-in-Law, Amos who had established his own Company, A. Davies & Co.

> **The Bankruptcy Act, 1869.**
> In the County Court of Cheshire, holden at Chester.
> In the Matter of a Special Resolution for Liquidation by Arrangement of the affairs of Robert Jones Davies, carrying on business under the style of R. J. Davies and Co., at Northgate-row, and the Roodee Works, in the city and borough of Chester, and formerly in partnership with John Rowlands Edwards and Elizabeth Edwards, and trading under the style or firm of R. J. Davies and Co., as Fruit Preservers and Manufacturing and Retail Confectioners, and residing at Hoole Park, in the county of Chester.
> JOHN PRICE, of No. 25, North John-street, in the city of Liverpool, Chartered Accountant, has been appointed Trustee of the property of the debtor. All persons having in their possession any of the effects of the debtor must deliver them to the trustee, and all debts due to the debtor must be paid to the trustee. Creditors who have not yet proved their debts must forward their proofs of debts to the trustee.—Dated this 21st day of July, 1883.

Thanks to the good offices of Malcolm John Davies of Boston, Lincolnshire, grandson of Isaac Davies of the Roodee Works, we now know the underlying reasons for these major changes in the Robert Jones Davies social and employment circumstances for, despite the large workforce and evident large volume of business, it is clear this was no longer profitable, as an entry in the London Gazette for 24th July 1883 shows that "The Bankruptcy Act, 1869, In the Matter of a Special Resolution for Liquidation by Arrangement of the affairs of Robert Jones Davies of Hoole Park, carrying on the business under the style of R. J. Davies & Co. at Northgate Row and the Roodee Works in the City & Borough of Chester and formerly in partnership with John Rowlands Edwards and Elizabeth Edwards etc."

On 25th September that year a notice was posted in the Gazette setting a deadline of 3rd October 1883 for Creditors to lodge their claims against the Company and send them to Messers Roose, Price & Co., 25, North John Street, Chartered Accountants, Liverpool, though unfortunately, we do not have any further details.

So Robert Jones Davies went into Voluntary Liquidation, which adequately explains all the problems, but it must have been a very difficult time for him

FIRST MEETINGS AND PUBLIC EXAMINATIONS—continued.

Debtor's Name.	Address.	Description.	Court.	No.	Date of First Meeting.	Hour.	Place.	Date of Public Examination.	Hour.	Place.	Date of Order, if any, for Summary Administration.
Carter, William Thomas	St. John's Ironworks, Bury St. Edmunds, Suffolk	Engineer and Boiler Maker	Bury St. Edmunds	4 of 1890	Feb. 28, 1890	12.15 P.M.	Office of Official Receiver, Ipswich	Mar. 5, 1890	11.45 A.M.	Guildhall, Bury St. Edmunds	
Day, Elizabeth Adelaide Wiseman	West-parade, Hythe, Kent, lately residing at 5, Linton-terrace, Hounslow, Middlesex	Spinster	Canterbury	73 of 1889	Mar. 7, 1890	10.30 A.M.	Official Receiver's Office, 5, Castle-street, Canterbury	Mar. 14, 1890	10.30 A.M.	Guildhall, Canterbury	Feb. 19, 1890
Gwilliam, Edwin	Maria Hill Stores, St. Paul's, and Moorfield House, St. Paul's, both in Cheltenham, Gloucestershire	Grocer and Provision Dealer	Cheltenham	6 of 1890	Mar. 1, 1890	8.80 P.M.	County Court-buildings, Cheltenham	Apr. 10, 1890	12 noon	County Court, Cheltenham	
Davies, Robert Jones (trading as R. J. Davies and Co.)	32, Duke-street, Chester, trading at the Roodee Works, Chester	Manufacturing Confectioner and Fruit Preserver	Chester	8 of 1890	Mar. 4, 1890	2.30 P.M.	Official Receiver's Offices, Crypt-chambers, Chester	Mar. 11, 1890	11 A.M.	The Castle, Chester	
Beaumont, Percy Frank	180, Fore-street, Exeter	Provision Dealer	Exeter	8 of 1890	Mar. 3, 1890	12 noon	Official Receiver's Offices, 18, Bedford-circus, Exeter	Mar. 13, 1890	11 A.M.	The Castle, Exeter	Feb. 18, 1890
Jardine, Emily Mary	Washfield Rectory, near Tiverton, Devonshire	Widow	Exeter	8 of 1890	Feb. 28, 1890	3 P.M.	The Castle, Exeter	Feb. 28, 1890	3.30 P.M.	The Castle, Exeter	Feb. 7, 1890
Nichols, Thomas	Hesketh Arms, Meadfoot-lane, Torquay, Devonshire	Innkeeper	Exeter	10 of 1890	Mar. 8, 1890	12 noon	Official Receiver's Offices, 18, Bedford-circus, Exeter	Mar. 13, 1890	11 A.M.	The Castle, Exeter	Feb. 18, 1890
Barber, George Arthur	St. Leonards-road, Mousehold, in the city of Norwich, lately residing and trading at Gorleston, Suffolk	Now out of business, lately Tin Plate Worker	Great Yarmouth	12 of 1890	Mar. 1, 1890	11 A.M.	Official Receiver's Office, 8, King-street, Norwich	Mar. 11, 1890	11 A.M.	Townhall, Great Yarmouth	
Fordick, Daniel Harry	The Albert Tavern, South Dene-road, Great Yarmouth, Norfolk, formerly the Half-way House Inn, Southtown, Suffolk	Licensed Victualler	Great Yarmouth	11 of 1890	Mar. 1, 1890	12 noon	Official Receiver's Office, 8, King-street, Norwich	Mar. 11, 1890	11 A.M.	Townhall, Great Yarmouth	Feb. 13, 1890
Watson, William James	5, Trinity-square, South Quay, Great Yarmouth, Norfolk, and Northgate-road, Great Yarmouth	Wheelwright	Great Yarmouth	13 of 1890	Mar. 1, 1890	11.30 A.M.	Official Receiver's Office, 8, King-street, Norwich	Apr. 15, 1890	11 A.M.	Townhall, Great Yarmouth	

socially, his being, according to the press report of his funeral, one of Chester's leading citizens, boss of a large business and a big churchman to boot, for bankruptcy was considered as near criminal conduct in those far off times and quite socially unacceptable.

It may also explain why he was not mentioned in Davies family circles as those with the knowledge were of the generation that still considered bankruptcy a social disgrace.

However, the County Court at Chester Castle, where the hearings were dealt with, evidently allowed him to continue trading, presumably in an attempt to pay off his creditors.

The London Gazette of 21st February 1890 notes Robert Jones Davies's Public Examination was to be held at the Official Receiver's Offices at Crypt Chambers, Chester on 11th March 1890.

On 14th March 1890 a Trustee was appointed by the Court, one John Ellis Edwards, Accountant of 29, Eastgate Row, Chester.

On 18th September 1891 Robert Jones Davies was still at 32, Duke St. and had paid one-shilling and two-pence ha'penny as Final Dividend though we do not know if this was the only payment or there had been others previously.

At this point the Roodee Works seems to have changed hands.

Chester Directory 1910 lists Robert Jones Davies as resident at 16, Eaton Road but he died of cancer on 3rd August of that year without leaving a Will and no records relating to his business affairs have been found. Interestingly, among the list of mourners at his funeral, admittedly incomplete, only his immediate family seems to have been present, there is no sign of any other family members, some close neighbours, who would almost certainly have been reported had they been there; a reflection of the bankruptcy perhaps?

The 1914 Directory lists Mrs. Davies as the householder and the property was still occupied by the family in 1920, as one of the daughters, Miss Edith Davies, died there that year and is buried in Chester Cemetery, but by 1923 the house was unoccupied, so those remaining had moved on, and when Margaret Elizabeth, known as 'Madge', died in 1956, she was living in Durban Avenue, Christleton; presently 14 and 16 Eaton Road are small hotels.

Robert Jones's wife, Jane (Chart 7), died in 1928 at Highfield, Stocks Lane, Chester, (still there), the home of her daughter Alessandrina McLellan, the family of Chester builders and drapers, and left a Will dated 1913 and her Estate of £3,629/1/11d (£3,629.10) to her two daughters, Madge and Edith but Edith died eight years earlier so it all went to Madge, worth some £175,000 in 2003.

Davies Sweet Shop, Watergate Street, Chester

Births

Amos Davies born in Brish Llanyonys Denbighshire in year 1841 on 17th February

Elen Davies born in Liverpool in year 1838

Marraged in St David church Liverpool

Children

Isaac Davies born in Elias Street Liverpool 15 April 1866
Crison St Christ church by Homer St Liverpool

Amos Jones Davies born Py croft Chester on 8th February 1868
Cryzon Sendebenkant Capel Pypers Parish St Mary

Richard Davies born Py Croft Chester 20 May 1869
Creson St Martin church

Robert Davies born in Wellington Row Hantridge Chester 27 February 1871
Crezon in St Bridget

Margret Elen Davies born September 1872
Mary Elizabeth Davies born 21st Jaunary 1875
Emaley Davies born October 9th 1877

3 Lort born in No 4 Roberts Court north gate Rd

Did April 20th 1882

Deaths

Emily Davies Brooks Works Chester	Died April 20= 1882
(Mother) Ellen Davies 15 City Road Chester	Died April 20= 1903

The family grave in Chester Old Cemetery, (Number 4511), is of great interest and reads :

"Robert J. Davies, Aug. 3rd. 1910, aged 74; Jane, wife of the above, Oct. 14th 1928, aged 84; also Margaret Elizabeth, eldest daughter, Jan. 13th. 1956, aged 89; also Edith Jane, 3rd. daughter 16th. June 1920, also Norah Gwendoline, daughter, died Jan. 3rd. 1887, aged 11 months, also their daughter Gladys Muriel Higham, July 1st.,1965, aged 83; also Donald Catherall McLellan, grandson, died 4th. Febuary 1904 aged 3 weeks; also their granddaughter Margaret Elizabeth Garnet Edwards, Oct. 8th. 1968, aged 59".

Dorothy at the grave of Robert Jones Davies and family at Chester Old Cemetery.

Robert Jones Davies, who could be called the Father of this Chester branch of the Davies family, was not the direct ancestor, that was his brother Amos, born 2nd February 1841, the third son and fourth child of Isaac and Margaret of Telpyn.

Amos only appears once in the early Census Returns and that for 1851, so the remaining times are a bit of a mystery until he reappears in Everton, Liverpool as a Labourer, marrying Ellen Rae, née Jones, a widow, at St. David's on 26th July 1865, her father being Richard Jones, a joiner. Family tales report that Amos went to sea, supported by the fact that he turned up in Liverpool, then a great port offering employment to many of those disillusioned by the grinding poverty of work on the land but extensive enquiries have failed to find Amos in Liverpool prior to his marriage, so we must assume the sea tales to be correct.

Judging by the places and dates of birth of their children, Amos and Ellen must have moved from Liverpool to Chester about 1867/8 to join his brothers, Isaac and Robert Jones, in the Confectionery business.

In 1871 Amos was living in Wellington Row, Handbridge (the six dwellings between Greenway Street

Amos

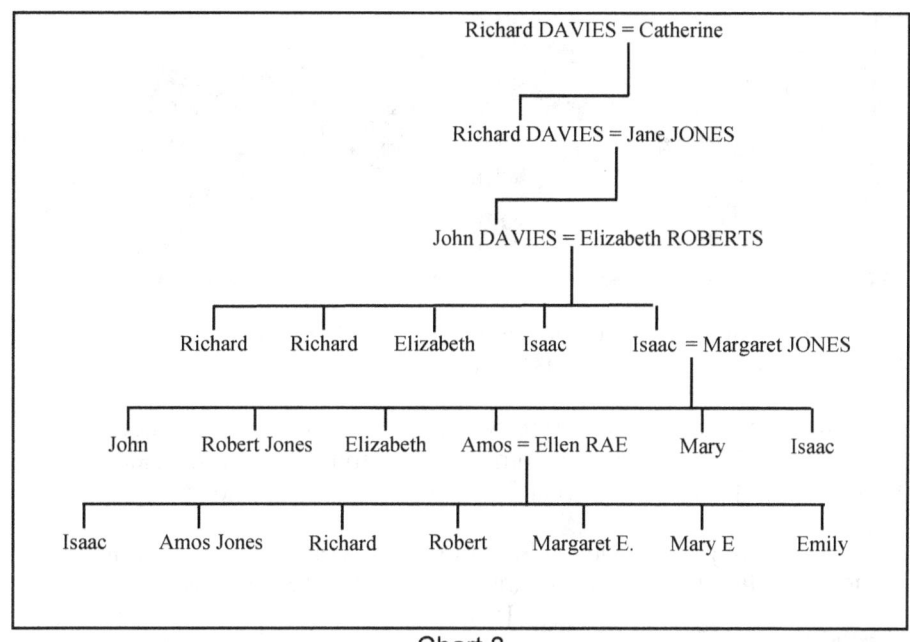

Chart 8

and the Grosvenor Arms) and managing a Company sweetshop at 11, Northgate Row though by 1896 this had moved to Number 7

On the census of 1881 Amos and Ellen and family were listed as living at the Roodee Works where they moved circa 1878 and where he was a warehouseman with children :

Amos Jones, aged 13;
Richard, aged 11;
Margaret, aged 8;
Mary Elizabeth, aged 5
and Emily, aged 3 who died aged 4½ years.

There was an elder son, Isaac, aged 15, not at home for the 1881 Census, who was born at Elias Street, Liverpool, and for reasons not understood, was brought up by his grandparents at Telpyn and, following leaving school, probably the National School at Llanhychan, he was employed at the Mill at Melin y Wern at Ash, eventually taking over the operation and retiring to Gwenallt, Abbey Road, Rhuddlan, where he died on 5th April 1945, leaving some £750,000 (in 2003 money) and is buried at Rhewl near his

Ellen

Pyecroft Street, Handbridge

Wellington Row

grandparents and his two wives, Anne, died 13th May 1902 aged 39 and Winifrid Lewis, died 1st April 1931, aged 52.

Amos Jones and Richard were born in the partly completed Pyecroft Street, Handbridge; Robert was born at Wellington Row; Margaret, Mary Elizabeth and Emily were born at 3, Robinsons Court, Northgate Street.

The Minute Book of Queen Street Congregational Church, (now mostly demolished though the facade is incorporated into Tesco's), records in an 1886 entry, that Richard Davies of Roodee a shop assistant, late of Christ Church, was 'converted', so the family was still at the Roodee Works and Richard was probably working at the Company sweetshop in Northgate Row. When the Roodee Works changed hands the family moved to 31, Watergate Street (now demolished).

Lizzie and Maggie

A Chester Directory for 1891 shows Amos living at 1, Trinity Street, (now demolished), and in 1892 having a shop in 5, Northgate Row, thereby a tenant of the famous Chester architect, John Douglas, who owned the site and des

By this time Amos had established his own Company, A. Davies & Co. and evidently taken over the lease of the Northgate shop from R. J. Davies & Co . later to expand the business to include shops in Watergate Street and Bridge Street where the operation was Wholesale and Retail.

There is no record of any possible transfer of business from the Roodee Works to Amos. In addition to the shops of A. Davies & Co. daughters Maggie and Lizzie lived in Bath Street and operated a sweetshop in Boughton, presumably purchasing stock from A. Davies & Co. They never married and later moved to 55, Tarvin Road where Maggie died on 8th April 1930, Lizzie then moved to live with her brother Isaac at Rhuddlan and died on 8th January 1934. Both are buried in the family grave in Chester Old Cemetery.

The 1896 and 1898 editions of Kelly's Directory of Chester show Amos with shops at 7, Northgate Row and 9, Watergate Street and living at 46, Bridge Street Row, where the cast iron kitchen range Ellen used is still in situ in the business there.

In the 1902 edition of Kelly's Directory, A. Davies & Co is listed as having a shop at 26, Bridge Street, being the central, street level shop of the three under the Dutch Houses. By 1906 Amos had retired and the business taken over by his sons Amos Jones and Richard and renamed R. Davies & Co.

The property at 26, Bridge Street was vacated by the Company in 1912 and then occupied by Harry Marston's cycle shop.

Isaac the Miller

Ellen died at 15, City Road, (now demolished), another sweet shop, 20th April 1903, so Amos went to live with his son Amos Jones and family at 22, Queen Street where he died on 8th November 1907, described as a Retired Confectioner, and is buried with Ellen in the family grave.

He left £620/16/1d, (about £35,000 in terms of 2003 money), and, in default of a Statement, it is assumed to be the value of the business as well as his personal effects.

When he made his Will in 1903 he was living at 79, Watergate Row, (now demolished), so yet another address in the eleven known over forty years, so life must have been far from settled.

Interestingly he only left £10 to his son Isaac the miller whereas the other four children received a quarter of the residue each.

The Miller's House

The Mill at Melin y Wern

The direct ancestor is Amos Jones and, living at 1, Trinity Street, (now demolished), with his parents, married Mary Elizabeth (Polly) Brown at Queen Street Church on 17th August 1891. Mary Elizabeth / Polly / Granny Davies, born we think on 21st Janury 1866 (?), although not strictly a Davies, her influence on the family and business was so profound that much effort has been expended in seeking her origins which, despite much research, remain a considerable mystery.

Her birth cannot be traced nor a Baptism, and she seems to have been acquired by a Mrs. Brown of 28, Stanley Terrace, Irlam Lane, Bootle, Liverpool and, at the age of about 15 months or earlier, she was fostered to a Mrs. Sarah Reeves, 12, Francis Street, Chester, widow; Mr. Reeves seems to have died in 1867 but the death cannot be traced locally.

The 1871 Census for that address records Polly as aged 5, an orphan, place of birth - 'not known'. There is no known link between Mrs. Brown and Mrs. Reeves but a possible clue in that Mrs. Brown's back garden joined that of a Maria Reeves from Cheshire so was this a relation and thereby the medium whereby Polly got to Chester?

Mrs. Brown and Polly

Among the family papers, unusually retained, is a series of 43 letters written by Mrs. Brown, who ran a Guest House, to Mrs. Reeves concerning Polly's welfare and the endearing tone and content of the letters suggests that Mrs. Brown may well have been Polly's mother and, for one reason or another, found it necessary to foster her out, far enough away from prying eyes but close enough to visit occasionally.

It has not been possible to trace Mrs. Brown prior to the start of the letters in 1867 nor trace her after the letters stopped.

In any event Polly was effectively brought up by Mrs. Reeves in Chester and the 1881 Census Return for 1, Back Brook Street (now demolished) reads :

Roderigo Hill, aged 35, general labourer;
his wife Sarah, aged 47;
Thomas, son, aged 6;
Mary Brown, dressmaker and adopted daughter, aged 15;
John Ray, a boarder, aged 42, a groom;
Frank Brooks, aged 30, a boarder and general labourer;
Alex Dixon, nephew, aged 25, boilermaker.

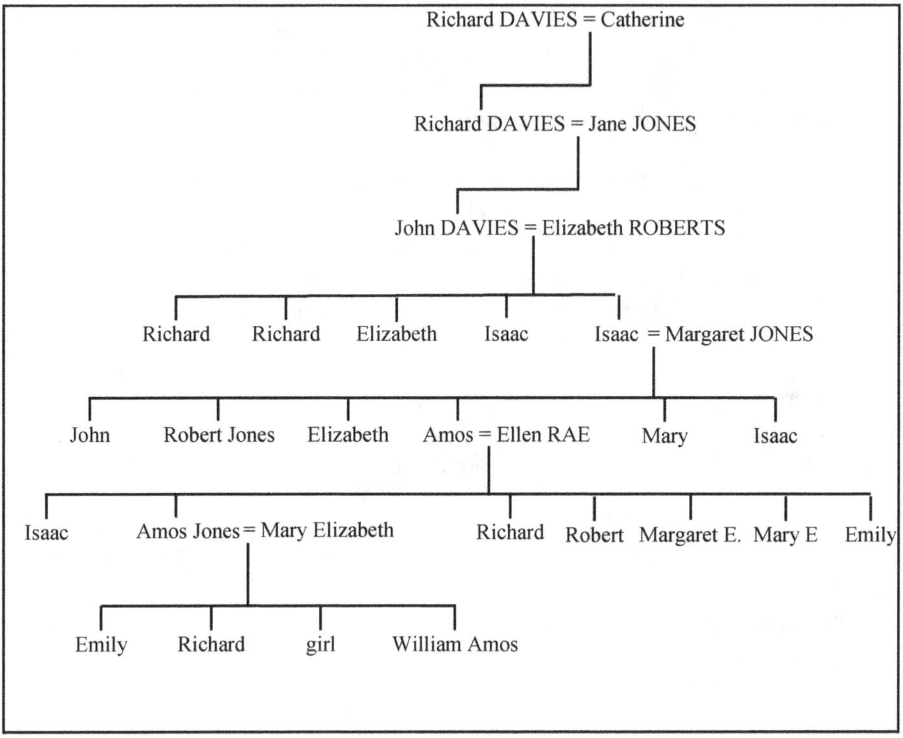

```
                  Richard DAVIES = Catherine
                           |
                  Richard DAVIES = Jane JONES
                           |
                  John DAVIES = Elizabeth ROBERTS
                           |
   ┌──────────┬──────────┬──────────┬──────────┐
 Richard   Richard   Elizabeth    Isaac    Isaac = Margaret JONES
                                                    |
          ┌──────────┬──────────┬──────────┬──────────┐
         John   Robert Jones  Elizabeth  Amos = Ellen RAE   Mary   Isaac
                                                |
   ┌──────────┬──────────────────┬──────────┬──────────┬──────────┬──────────┐
 Isaac   Amos Jones = Mary Elizabeth    Richard   Robert  Margaret E.  Mary E   Emily
                |
      ┌──────────┬──────────┬──────────┐
    Emily    Richard     girl    William Amos
```

Chart 9

So Mrs. Reeves had remarried to Roderigo Hill but the 1891 Census for 28, Talbot Street records some more bad news :
 Mrs. Sarah Hill, widow ;
 Thomas Hill, stepson;
 George Spruce, railway worker;
 Mary Elizabeth Brown, adopted daughter.

Sarah Reeves and Her Husband

When Mrs. Reeves made her Will in 1888 she was living at 28, Talbot Street and left everything to her adopted daughter Polly and signed her name with an 'X', though it is not clear from this if she was illiterate or just acting according to the prejudices of the times.

Adoption at that time was rather a vague term applied when occasion was thought necessary to almost any child who was not a family member and happened to have been taken into the household for all sorts of reasons, it was not the exact term it later became following the 1926 Adoption Act. Prior to her marriage to Amos Jones, Polly had a dressmaking business located above Becketts the drapers in Eastgate Row.

When Polly died on 10th July 1954 documents were discovered by her children which evidently shed some light on her origins but, very unfortunately, the material was considered too sensitive for the rest of the family to see so was destroyed!

The marriage of Mary Elizabeth and Amos Jones produced four children as shown on Chart 9:
Emily, 21st May 1892 to 7th February 1982.
Richard, 18th April 1895 to 12th March 1954.
Girl, (stillborn) March 1898.
Wiliam Amos, 25th February 1902 to 14th March 1978.

A.J. Davies 'Caer' Works, Chester

William Amos Davies in York Street, circa 1913
William Amos on cart, brother Richard in Bowler

Emily was born at 6, St. Martin's Ash (now demolished) at the south-west end of Nicholas Street. Richard was born at 15, Nicholas Street (now demolished). William Amos was born at 30a, Watergate Row. In 1902 Amos and Polly moved into 8, Queen's Avenue purchased by Polly in 1897 and rented out for seven shillings a week.

In 1907 Richard withdrew his Bank Guarantee due to some professional problem with his brother Amos Jones, so the partnership was broken up and Richard continued to operate R. Davies & Company and Amos Jones and Polly set up a partnership styled A. J. Davies & Co., purchasing a property at 1a, York Street, previously a brush factory, where they established a wholesale confectionery warehouse, eventually incorporating a boiled sweet factory called Deva Confectionery.

The business traded under the name of 'Queen', the logo depicting Queen Alexander, so it must have been introduced in 1902 or thereabouts, and the property carried the name A. J. Davies Queen Confectionery Works.

Some time prior to February 1919 the name 'Queen' was dropped and a logo adopted depicting the Walls of Chester surrounding the word 'CAER', the Welsh name for Chester, no doubt taking into account the Welsh family background and the many Welsh customers who made up the greater part of the business.

Due to space considerations Deva Confectionery had moved to 46, Frodsham Street circa 1910 and moved back to York Street after The Second World War.

In domestic terms the family seems to have moved from 30a, Watergate Street to 22, Queen Street by 1907 when Amos died there.

They were still there in the 1910 edition of the Chester Directory but by the 1914 edition had moved down the road to 28, Queen Street, which was purchased about that time, along with 1a, York Street, both properties being a part of the block containing 1a, York Street / Back Queen Street where the confectionery business was located.

On the occasion of their 25th wedding anniversary Amos Jones and Polly, having had at least seven previous addresses, made their final move to Manor House, Queen's Park, which became the focus for the Davies family social life until sold in 1968, when Emily and Jake moved to Kilmorey Park, Hoole (Emily and Jake are described in Chapter Two)..

In 1918 A. J. Davies & Company and, presumably, Deva Confectionery Company, became Limited Companies with all the family members serving as Directors from time to time. The War Office was asked to expedite the demob of Richard Davies from the Army where he was serving in the Royal Army

A.J Davis & Co Ltd. First van FM 128 with Aunt Em at Ruthin

Medical Corps, Official Number 83602, and he rejoined the Company in 1919. Directors meetings were held at Manor House until 1944, thereafter at York Street.

The York Street properties were owned by Polly who rented them to the Company for the sum of £30 per year. The Company accountant was initially Walter Baird and later Haswell Bros. Banking was originally with the Chester branch of the Liverpool Bank Ltd, (south-east corner of St. Werburgh's Street), later changed to Barclays Bank Ltd.

Amos Jones' brother Richard left Chester circa 1923 and his wholesale business was purchased by A. J. Davies for £150 plus commission of 3.75% on cash outstanding sales; his shops were sold to R. Turnhill & Co.

A telephone was installed in York Street in August 1919 and the firm's first commercial motor vehicle, an ex-military 20 hp Ford ambulance, FM 1285, was purchased in February 1919 for the sum of £280; the same year a new 17/25 hp Dodge van, FM 1354, was purchased for £500 with a further example, FM 1654, following shortly after.

In June 1921 the Company purchased an AC Cyclecar for £48 18shillings (£48.90). During this period concern was expressed about old stock, some of which included laces, balloons, lunch cubes (?) and pills.

1923 saw falling prices so the reduced turnover caused some concern. In 1926 the rebuilding and enlargement of 1a, York Street was funded by Polly. Amos Jones died on 19th October 1927 aged 59 and is buried in Chester New Cemetery; he suffered poor health all his life, mainly diabetes.

World War Two came along on 3rd September 1939 and, as in the previous World War, produced severe sugar rationing with an allocation of Personal Points for the purchase of a very limited amount of sweets; additionally a limit on profits made trading very difficult.

The war period also produced critical shortages of personnel, petrol, food and most consumer items, nearly all of which were rationed.

W.A. Davies, Official Number 1884405, was called up for the Royal Air Force and served a year and a day, being allocated a wage of £8 a week whilst serving.

Deva Confectionery, in the boiling shop in York Street, was closed down in 1955 and the shares purchased by A. J. Davies & Co. Ltd.

Sometime in the past the Company had acquired, by way of a bad debt, a sweet shop at 31, Brook Street and, for some unknown reason, considered that it should be owned by one of the family so it was sold to W. A. Davies for £256/-/7d (£256.03) in 1941.

It was named The Dorothy Confectionery Company and traded as The Dorothy Box, subsequently being sold on in 1955 to G & A Thompson who continued trading until the whole block was demolished to accommodate the road 'improvements' of the Inner Ring Road; the site in now under the Gaumont roundabout.

The Dorothy Box, Brook Street, Chester

In 1947 the property at 3, (later 5), Bold Place, Chester was purchased by the Company from Mr. Millwood for £1,000 and, two years later, sold to Ward Jones for £1,100. Another purchase was the wholesale confectionery business of B. Harrison, who traded from Mason Street, the stocks were transferred to York Street together with Mr. Harrison who then became a sales-rep for A. J. Davies & Co. Ltd.

May 1950 saw the purchase of a Triumph Renown car for W. A. Davies, LFM 920 at a cost of £996/10/7d, (£996.53), and November of the same year a Ford V8 Pilot, MFM 734 was purchased for R. Davies at a cost of £806/8/-d, (£806.40).

END OF SWEET RATIONING

How The Public Can Co-operate

Observer 1953

STATEMENT BY MR RICHARD DAVIES

Mr. Richard Davies, of A. J. Davies and Co., Ltd., manufacturing confectioners, York-street, Chester, vice-president of both the Wholesale Confectioners' Alliance and the British Federation of Wholesale Confectioners, took part in the negotiations between the Industry and the Ministry of Food prior to Monday's announcement that the rationing of all chocolates and sweets will end on 24th April. He met Mr. Strachey in London last Friday.

Mr. Davies, who is chairman of the Finance Committee, Chester City Council, in an interview on Tuesday before leaving Chester again for London, said "There will not be an unlimited supply of sweets available after 24th April, but it is the aim of the industry, in conjunction with the Ministry, to make available during the first four weeks of de-rationing an amount of at least 5½oz. per head per week. The industry and the Ministry anticipate that the supplies to follow this will be almost sufficient to meet full consumer demands. The success of de-rationing in the initial stage will really depend on the co-operation of the general public. If everyone rushes to obtain supplies during the first few days of de-rationing, it will cause queues outside the shops. If people will just obtain their requirements as they want them from day to day or week to week during the first few weeks, there will be sufficient sweets in the shops for everybody" he said

York Street circa 1913 William Amos

Queen Street circa 1913 Left to right: Mr and Mrs Harding, Richard, Amos Jones, Polly, William Amos

In 1953, due to the increase in business following the lifting of sweet rationing together with handling problems at York Street, consideration was given to moving to a site on the Chester Trading Estate where the operation would be on one floor, however this idea was scrapped and the existing warehouse extended into 29, Queen Street and 1a, York Street, properties owned by the Company and previously tenanted.

Polly died on 10th July 1954 and was buried in Chester New Cemetery.

On 1st July 1934, Emily Davies, warehouse manager at York Street, married Gordon Robert Jacob (known as 'Jake) at Upton by Chester Congregational Chapel, there no children of the marriage.

They set up home with Polly at Manor House, eventually purchasing the property following extensive bomb damage on 7th April 1941 when a HE bomb exploded opposite Manor House, one of many HE and incendiary bombs that dropped across Queen's Park that night.

Despite having an air raid shelter in the front garden, no-one was in it, however there were no casualties.

Jake went on to found a timber and forestry business, J. R. Gordon & Co., in Newgate Street and died in hospital in 1982,

Polly and Amos Jones

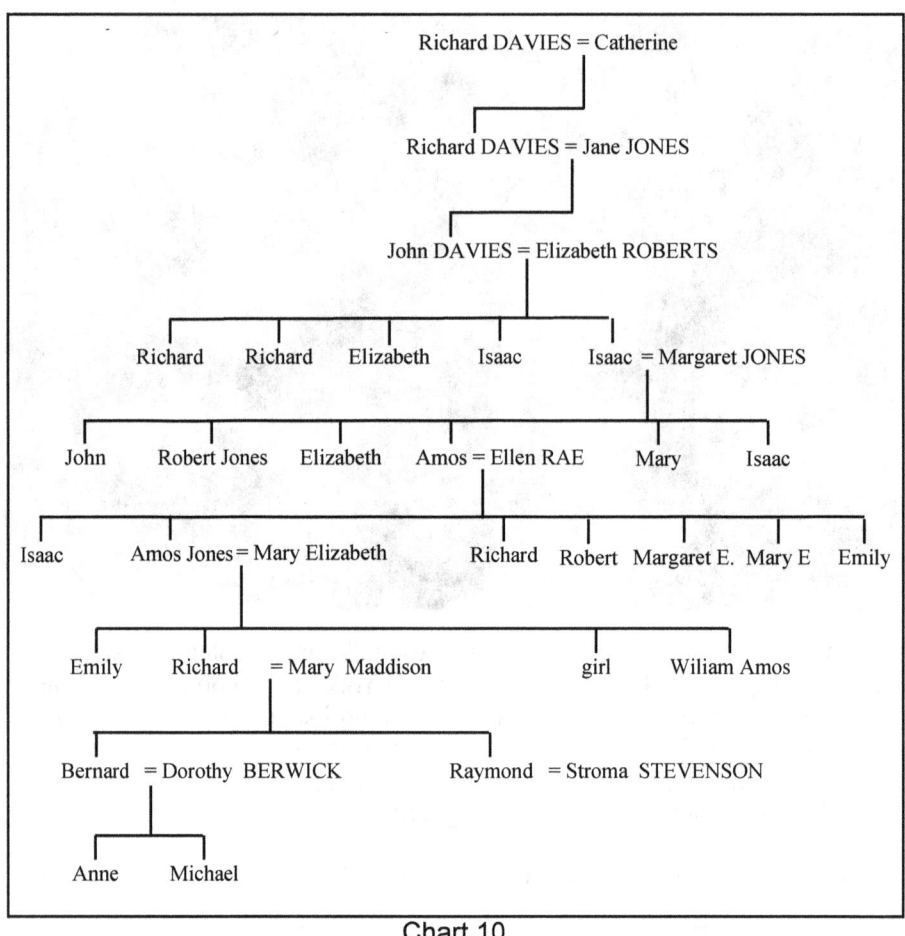

Chart 10

the same year that Emily died, also in hospital, following a fall in St. Werburgh's Street.

William Amos' brother Richard married Mary Maddison at Queen St. Church in September 1917, presumably whilst he was on leave from the R.A.M.C. Mary was born in Farndon on 13th April 1892. They set up home in a house owned by Polly at 12, Churton Street.

Latterly they moved to Southend, then Lyndale, both in Queen's Park; there were two children of the marriage, Raymond and Bernard.

Richard was a Director of A. J. Davies & Co. Ltd and active on Chester City Council for many years, latterly as Chairman of the Finance Committee and Sheriff 1952/3.

Richard died on 12th March 1954 and Mary in 1968.

Bernard

Raymond

DEATH OF MR. AMOS J. DAVIES.

Former Chester Tradesman.

It is with regret that we record the death, which occurred on Wednesday, of a well-known Chester tradesman and a prominent Freemason, Mr. Amos Jones Davies, of Manor House, Queen's Park, Chester. Mr. Davies, who was 60 years of age, was a native of Chester and was a manufacturing confectioner, having a warehouse at York-street, which was taken over some time after the retirement of his father over 20 years ago.

Mr. Davies' father, Mr. Amos Davies, was also a well-known Chester tradesman and formerly lived in Bridge-street Row over the shop where he carried on business. He also had business premises in Northgate-street and Watergate-street.

Mr. Amos Jones Davies and his brother, Mr. R. Davies, managed the Watergate-street and Bridge-street shops, respectively, upon the death of their father, and it was Mr. Amos Jones Davies who opened and developed the manufacturing side of the business at the York-street premises.

He had been a Freemason for the past 20 years, and was a member of the Travellers' Hunter-street. Mr. Davies leaves a widow, two sons, and one daughter. The sons, Mr. A. W. Davies and Mr. R. Davies, are both in the York-street business. His wife was formerly Miss M. E. Brown, a native of Chester.

FUNERAL OF MR. A. J. DAVIES.—The funeral of Mr. Amos Davies, of Manor House, Queen's Park, whose death was reported last week, took place on Friday last week, when the remains were cremated at the Liverpool Crematorium. The family mourners were: Mrs. A. J. Davies (widow), Messrs. R. Davies and A. W. Davies (sons), Miss E. Davies (daughter), Messrs. R. Davies and I. Davies (brothers), Miss M. E. Davies (sister), Mrs. M. Davies (daughter-in-law), Mr. Maddison, Miss Loan, Miss Johnson, Mr. Campbell, Mr. and Mrs. Mansley, Mr. and Mrs. Proud, Mr. and Mrs. Baird and Miss Baird, Mr. C. Rowley, Mr. A. Hughes (Holywell), Mr. Hurstfield (Crewe), Mr. D. C. Davies, Mr. Robinson and Miss Robinson (Liverpool), Mr. A. Eden, Mr. Brown, Mr. and Mrs. Garnett, Mr. J. Barton (Wolverhampton), Mr. W. Barton, Messrs. V. Cain, F. Brown, H. Hesketh and E. Sconce (employes of Messrs. A. J. Davies and Co., Ltd.), Messrs. J. Bibb, T. A. Jones, C. Bibb, C. Lanceley and F. Smith (representing the confectionery trade), Mr. Stone (Farndon), Mr. Hutchinson (Chester) and Mr. A. Williams (Chester).

Their son Bernard joined the firm immediately following war service in radar in the Royal Air Force, Official Number 2203141, and married Dorothy Berwick in 1945; there were two children, Anne and Michael.

Raymond served in the Army for the duration of the war, Official Number 2091488, latterly as Captain; he married Stroma Stevenson at Haddington in 1952 and worked for a time at York Street; there were no children.

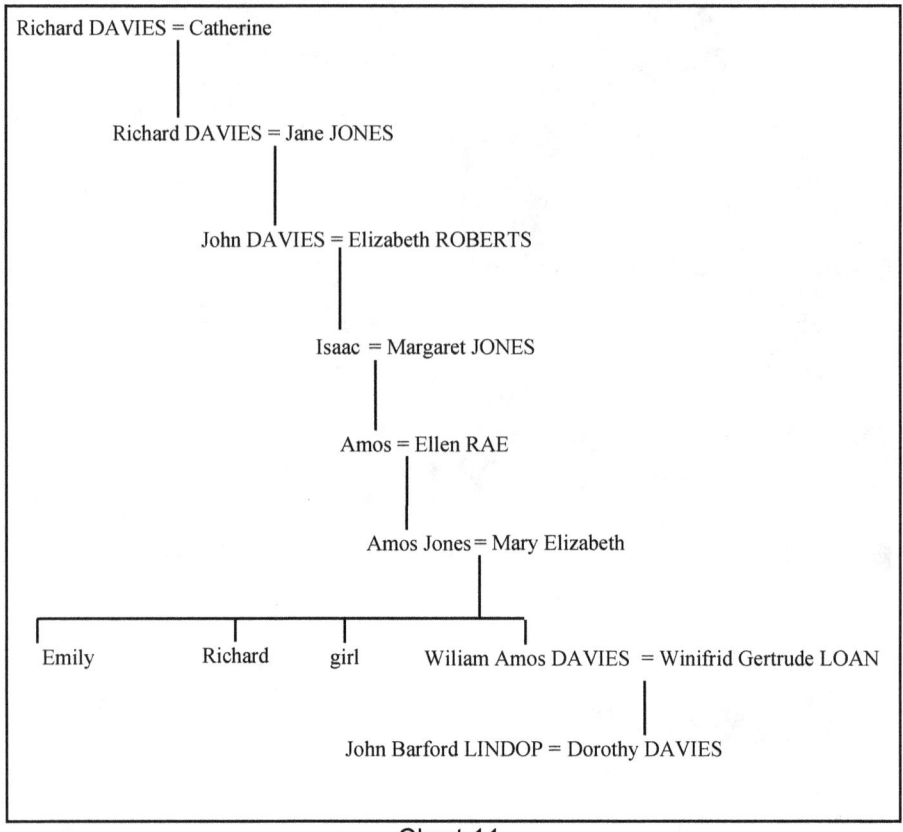

Chart 11

Wiliam Amos married Winifrid Gertrude Loan, (born Leeds, 7th April 1897), at Queen Street Church on 10th September 1928; he was Chairman. and Managing Director of A. J. Davies & Co. Ltd and very active in voluntary work in Chester. He died 14 March 1978.

There was one daughter Dorothy, who worked for the business following leaving school until her marriage to John Lindop, (who served in radar in the Royal Navy, Official No. D/JX 540875), at Upton Congregational Church on 30th June 1954; there were three children, Jean, Zoe and Robert. After the Second World War various firms were acquired by A. J. Davies & Co. Ltd: Corbetts of Oswestry, Bebbingtons of Chester and the Crown Confectionery of Birkenhead.

After the deaths of William Amos and Richard the management of the firm was continued by Bernard and finally wound up and the business and property sold in 1989. Presently the building has been refurbished as an office block.

Richard Davies (left) and his wife Mary (right), His friend Keith-Hill is in the centre.

Picture taken circa 1953

Dorothy with her parents

Aunt Em and Jake

Aunt Em (Emily Jacobs nee Davies) was the nearest the family had to an historian with the added benefit of living in the ancestral home at Manor House, Queens Park, Chester where all the surviving Davies records and memorabilia were kept.

Em knew of the Roodee Works but it is not clear if she was aware of the actual significance to the Davies story as she never mentioned Robert Jones Davies nor the location of the Works. Some material relating to R.J. Davies & Co. The Chester Preserving Company and the Roodee Works had survived at Manor House but, inexplicably, Emily threw it out.

In so far as contact with the family of Robert Jones Davies was concerned Emily knew the McLellan family and was aware to some degree that Alessandrina McLellan née Davies was a close relation but there is some doubt if she was aware that Alessandrina was a daughter of Robert Jones. Additionally she had contact with Gladys Muriel Higham and Margaret Elizabeth Garnet Edwards, daughters of Robert Jones daughter Gladys, and was again aware of some close family relationship but how close is not known. She was also very friendly with the Missess Davies of Lache Park Avenue, two daughters of D.C. Davies of Dee, Cestrian and Laycock, the mineral water manufacturers of Linenhall Street, later in Station Road.

It may well be that there is a link here with David Evan Davies of Telpyn whose ancestor had been the manager of a soda water plant in Ruthin and it seems very likely that the Missess Davies were family members but from several generations back.

Gordon Robert Jacobs .
Known to the family as 'Jake', he was born at Kidsgrove in 1900 and clearly of Middle East extraction, probably Semitic, maybe Jewish, but professed to know

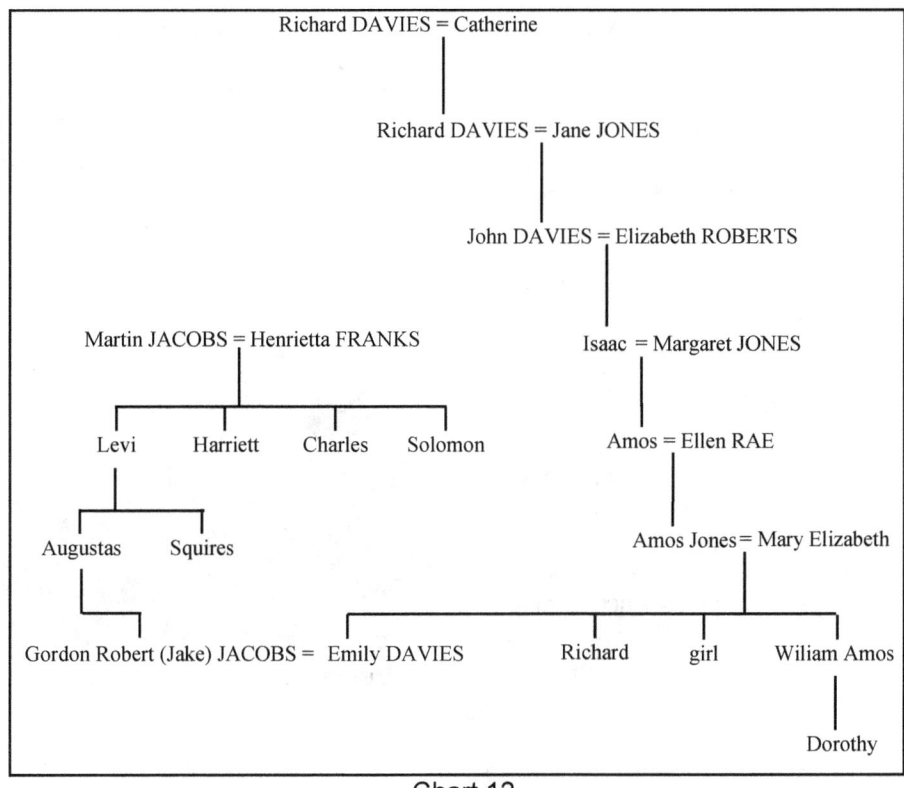

Chart 12

nothing of his origins other than that of his father, Augustus Jacobs, some hazy links with Liverpool and a comment about being in the ladder business.

It was therefore decided to look into the family background and see what could be discovered. His ancestors were found in the various Census Returns for Liverpool, commencing with the 1841 edition as well as in various Trade and Street directories.

His great great grandparents were Martin Jacobs and his wife Henrietta, neé Franks, who emigrated from Ovelgonne, near Hamburg, Germany, some time about 1825.

They first appear in London about that date, probably already married, and where the first child, Levi, was born, to be followed by two more.

Around 1833 the family moved to Liverpool where further children were born and Martin was a French Polisher and much involved in the Jewish community there.

Solomon Jacobs was born to Martin and Henrietta at 7.00 AM on 14th February 1840 at the family home at St. David's Place and Martin signed the

Birth Certificate with an 'X' and a mysterious set of numbers, '8. 3. 2371' or similar which, do not relate to the Jewish Calendar and so far have defied interpretation. Following the death of Martin his wife carried on the French Polishing business, added trading in flawed fabrics known as 'fents' (the nearest modern term to fents are remnants although these do not normally contain faults). At some later stage Henrietta taught languages.

She was evidently then living, until her own death in 1874, with a daughter Harriet who was married to a Hungarian Jew called Sinyaberger, also a French Polisher.

The eldest son, Levi, (Jake's grandfather), was, according to family tales, Chief Rabbi in Liverpool and by profession a cigar maker ; he married twice and died the same year as his mother. The only child of the second marriage was Squires who became the Managing Director of Avery Scales where Jake's father, Augustus, worked for some years as a rep.

Manor House, Queen's Park,

Augustus married at the C of E Church at Everton where Jake was baptised and, after he left Avery Scales, worked for the Shropshire Union Canal Co. in Chester where Jake was also employed for a time.

Prior to marrying Emily Davies in 1934, Jake worked for the Canal Company then moved into Insurance and lived at home, Deva Terrace, Chester.

From Insurance he moved into Forestry and Timber but it has not been possible to discover what prompted that move. The business he founded was J. R. Gordon & Co., Timber Merchants with offices at 14/16, Newgate Street, Chester. The prime activity of the firm was Forestry with Mills in North and Mid Wales and operational sites at Celyn, Willaston, Cynwyd, Northop, Llandovery, Newtown and sundry other units of a less permanent nature, plus, latterly, the prestigious Board Mill at Pentre, Queensferry. The Company was sold to the Powel Duffryn Group in 1956 for £61,000 or about £1M in 2003 money.

Jake continued to manage the business until his retirement in 1959 and for some years following sat on various committees relating to Forestry and lived on the Capital from the sale of the business.

By the time they died in 1982 most of that Capital had been spent, a large amount of it supporting many members of his family in a most generous manner.

Wedding Guests and other relatives

The full page wedding photo is that of Richard Davies, brother of Amos Jones, and Elizabeth Clegg who are in the centre of the photo.

The photograph was taken at the residence of the bride, Waterworks House, a property within the Chester Waterworks grounds at Boughton where she lived with her Uncle, George Crowe, a Chester

Dorothy stands in front of Waterworks House

Waterworks employee in some senior capacity, thought to be Chief Engineer or similar.

Parson Wynne Evans from Queen Street Chapel is in the doorway to the rear and the remainder are mostly the relatives of the brides family; there is also a possibility that one or more of Robert Jones sons are there as well. Following the wedding Richard and Elizabeth made a home at Newry Lodge, 42, Hoole Road, Chester where two children were born, Lillian and Arthur Leslie. Lillian married the son of the minister of Queen Street Church, Oswald Hilts, who held a Pilot's licence from World War 1 and was a senior

The full unmarked copy of the above photograph is shown on Page 2

figure in the Air Transport Auxiliary (ATA) ferrying service aircraft during the Second World War.

There were two daughters of the marriage, Patrica and Elizabeth.

Kelly's Directory of Chester for 1923 shows the family still at Hoole Road but the 1924 edition shows a Norton family in residence, so by then the Davies family had moved to Golders Green Road, Hendon.

The son, Arthur-Leslie, died of gas poisoning at home in Hendon, aged 22, but whether it was deliberate or an accident could not be determined.

Granny Davies

Granny Davies was very friendly with the Barton family in Chester and contact with a surviving member told that Polly lived with them for some time before her marriage to Amos Jones.

All the relevant Census Returns show her to be living with the Reeves/Hills so the precise reasons, when and where she was with the Bartons, are yet more mysteries.

Elizabeth & Richard

McLellan

The McLellan family was relevant to the history of both the Davies and Lindop families.

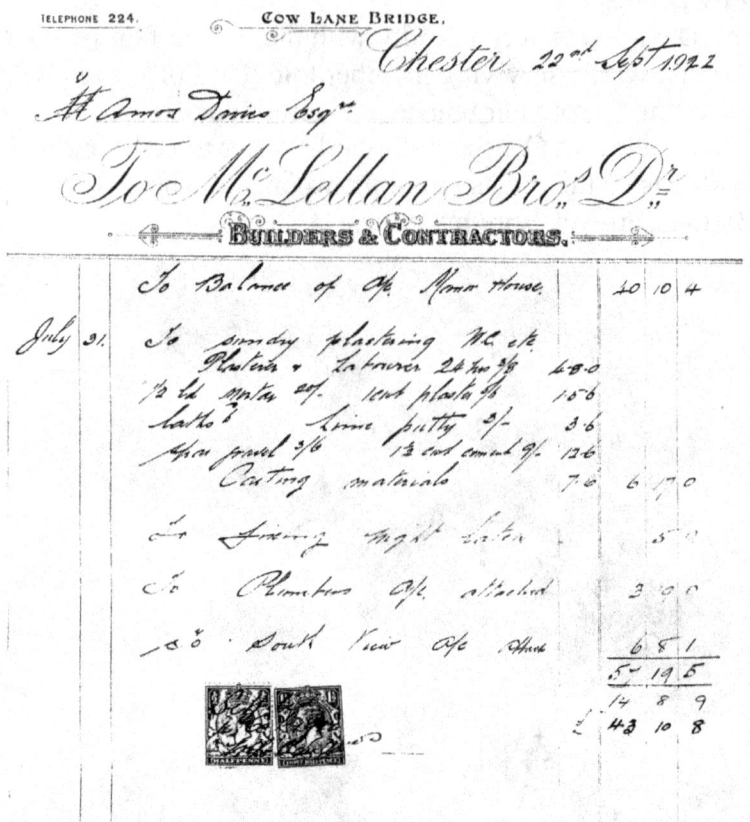

George and Mary McLellan were domiciled in a village near Alloa in Stirlingshire and were the parents of George, (1802-1879), and Alexander Flint, (1803-1865).

The brothers arrived in Chester *circa* 1830 and opened a draper's shop in Eastgate Row South in property rented from Bollands.

George married Mary Catherall at Bunbury 25th December 1833 and they had several children, one of whom was Alexander Flint, (1841-1893) who married Emma Rowe on 11th July 1863 and their sixth child was Richard Catherall McLellan, (1874-1945); he was a Builder and Contractor in Chester and lived in Stocks Lane.

He married Alessandrina Davies, (1875-1947), a daughter of Robert Jones Davies, brother of Amos Davies, Dorothy Lindop's great grandfather.

Alexander Flint, (1841-1893), would have been the surviving brother running the draper's shop when it was sold in 1883 to William Edward Lindop, his former apprentice. W.E. Lindop was John Barford Lindop's grandfather.

Welsh Placenames

Davies:	derives from Davy, ie:son of David.
Ruthin:	Red Town, from the colour of the soil.
Rhos:	A Moor.
Rhewl:	A Road.
Hwylfa:	A Lane.
Melin y Wern:	Mill in the Meadow/Marsh/Alder Grove.
Maesmaencymro:	Field of the Welsh stone.
Pontilen:	Llens (Ellens) bridge.
Clwyd:	A Gateway.
Abergele:	Mouth of the River Gele (Gele meaning a sword or blade).
Telpyn:	A piece of land.
Trevechan:	Small (minor) village.
Bryncaredig:	Kindly hill.
Llan:	A church, originally an enclosure.
Llanbedr:	Church of St. Peter.
Llanhychan:	Church of St. Hychan.
Llanelwy:	Church on the River Elwy (Elwy meaning bends or turns).
Llandygai:	Church of Tegai (a personal name).
Llangynhafal:	Church of St. Cynhafal (a 7th. Century Saint).
Llanfurog:	Church of Mwrog (a personal name).
Llandyrnog:	Church of St. Dyrnog.
Llanfair Duffryn:	Church of St. Mary in the Valley.
Llanfairfechan:	Church, small (ie;outpost of a larger unit), of St.Mary.
Llanynys:	Leland writes in 1540 *'It is caullid Llaneinys by cause the Chirch is set betwixt the Ryvers Cluid and Clwydog as in an Isle'*.
Ynys	usually translates as Isle, sometimes Watermeadow.

John Barford Lindop's book *Lindop: A Family History* published by Mercianotes charts his own genealogy.
For details visit **http://www.mercianotes.com**

www.ingramcontent.com/pod-product-compliance
Lightning Source LLC
Chambersburg PA
CBHW070347120426
42742CB00054B/2595